Vulnerabilities

Vulnerabilities

Boby Techi

DAMICK PUBLICATIONS

DAMICK PUBLICATIONS

Website: www.damickpublications.com
Email: damickpublications@gmail.com
Contact: +91-9999212301

First Published by Damick Publications 2023

ISBN: 978-81-964026-7-9

I will wait patiently, to find my words again,
to clear my head of the noise outside, of impending
expectations, the desire for perfection.

CONTENTS

COURAGE

INHIBITION

i want to hold on so tight
that I think of letting go

Chains

Sometimes I wish I was laughing amongst a hundred people like it was nothing.
Sometimes I wish I could show up anywhere on a whim.
I wish my mind didn't have chains.

i haven’t been embracing myself for so long

i want to

Pleas

Some words never leave my mouth.
If you could read my eyes,
you'd find a thousand pleas.

i am in my head a lot

Do you ever think of me

You are a free soul, I am not.
You walk with your dreams, I only dream.
You smile at everyone, while I shy away.
And this is why I wonder
how it'll feel like to be near you,
so close I can hear your thoughts
that are locked up inside your crowded mind.

i yearn for a slow life
stretching my arms while I smile

Drowning in me

How can I give you love when I have nothing inside.
I am plain as a plain sheet of paper,
I have no dimension no warmth.
I am a dark, cold body drowned in itself.
So forgive me, for not doing enough.

am i any good?
why do I keep falling back to this question

A voice i'll never forget

Constantly trying.
Trying my best to fit in.
To laugh like them
to talk like them
to belong with them.

I speak to myself when i'm all alone,
I am my solace my keeper
I am my comforter when everything feels harsh.

I am my warm hug.

how
did
I
end up here

Shells

Devoid of emotions
we are but shells,
deeply buried
we swim in our own sea.

LOVE

your thought is like wallpaper in my head

Air and Earth

He was like the wind
and I was the cold ground.
He'd never stay still
while I struggled to come out.

some pictures make me wish I never grew up
can I have that day again
that particular day

Bruno

Bruno.
You were our first love our first kid.
The fish shaped mark on your body was our favourite.
We grew up together, although with time; your waiting period kept extending.
From hours to weeks to months.
Eventually we left home only to visit once every year.

How hard it must've been for you,
to always see us leaving,
returning each time a little different—

I remember one of your days too when you suddenly looked old;
your hair turned grey.

If only I could see you again,
To say goodbye.
To say *sorry.*

Bruno. Our forever love.

love doesn’t want to make me write
as much as pain does

Trails of love

As I walked towards sending you off
I could see trails of love marking down your path.
It was a short trip with varied experiences— sun, people, houses,
occasional cars, the mushy grass that had me walking barefoot.
I looked up and saw these beautiful trees beneath which
you were laid,
it was beautiful.

if someone asks me
what do i tell them

i don't know who i am

A spring evening

The cold flew away,
sweaters are going back,
leaves turning green
so tenderly pleasing.
Nostalgia won't leave me,
it followed me through the lighted street.

nobody needs to know the story behind your places

To my lover

We have our own little world
that we carry with us,
you are my home when I am with you.
Your eyes console me.

we will always remain the people we were in pictures

CC

The only solace I have is that I loved you.
Never wished for eternity but your time
felt like sand in my hand,
slipping away as I desperately held on to it.

Time doesn't pass, it doesn't heal,
You are still here
We, are still here.

people are beautiful
when they are their bare selves

A far off cliff

There are times when I feel a void between us.
Like you'll never know how I feel about certain things.
Things that are a part of me, things that made me.
You see me just from the surface,
you listen to my story from a far off cliff
where I have to shout for you to hear it.

Will you ever reach this side?
Where we talk with our hearts and not with our words,
that day, we will truly be one.

the long nights with you
the early mornings too

These moments

And I miss you. I miss your casual kindness towards me.
Thinking of me even when you aren't consciously.
I miss your rush your chaos your laugh, I miss your sporadic entry into the room mumbling something, I miss your questions that I ignore, I miss you looking at me with softness in your eyes, I miss your tired body lying next to mine and your warm hands that comfort me and hold me against your chest.

Everything disappears except these moments when I miss you.

sadness clings to me no matter where I am
or what i'm doing
it is plastered all over me

You're gone

The last drive away from you.
The last time i'll be leaving you.
The next time you won't be here,
you're gone.

i miss when things were
simpler

when just being you was
enough

Admirer

I have been silently watching
your soft heart, your gentle approach,
towards the things you love.
How you stand for what you believe in
even if it hardly makes a difference.
You seem *sorted* out, untangled; with no urgency.
It makes me want to know you better.

CRISIS

everything is damp
there's no air no light

It's hard to articulate myself

I can feel you drifting away,
your voice is different
your pause is not the same.

the thought of nostalgia never occurred before
now we live to create memories

Distorted reality

I never learned to love,
just lived without it.
Blinded by reality
I never looked beyond it.

you want so much from others
because you give so little to yourself

It doesn't cost a dime to put a smile

You were there with all the lights,
and I was here.
Thinking all that mattered were the big things,
where have we disappeared
why have we forgotten
to celebrate our *small wins?*

to some
solitude is a mere word
to me
it is my whole world

Nowhere

I'm missing home
but I have nowhere to go,
no one to be with.
I miss a place that doesn't exist for me,
I miss a place where i'll be happy.
A place where I reach and my body leaves a big sigh of relief
where I can be me without being judged,
I miss a place like that.
A place where there are no rules,
no obligation to be a certain way,
a place that doesn't deplete my energy,
a place where fear won't find me.

I miss this place so much.

the humility to accept defeat will open up your heart

I am no better

Envy is like a hungry child,
it demands to be fed.
It satiates itself after you've spewed dirt and hate,
it keeps you on the edge,
not dying but never really living.

can't you be a still lake
with
gentle ripples

Quicksand

You vomit on my flowers.
You are an overcast on my hopes,
you drown me in your lake of misery;
just when I was starting to look at the sun.

there is a side that we keep to ourselves
protecting it like a child
we never let it leave

Spider

I would stay in my room for a week
without seeing daylight.
People scared me.
I don't remember how I spent my time
but I remember the fear and the mess,
the dreams and the stillness,
the orange walls that I do not wish to go back to,
the days where I felt nothing
didn't know the difference between surviving and living.
I was a spider webbing my own dreams with no one around.
What was I doing
what was I thinking.
I'm glad it's over
it's all gone.

i’m floating above your conversations
looking from the outside
trying to make sense

Resolve

I can't do world
it exhausts me.

i was always afraid
to be myself

Drunk

She tried to be kind to me.
But I was in a different dimension,
I couldn't read kindness.
I feel like most of my life I was drunk
and I couldn't see things for what they were.
I wasn't present enough to interpret the good
things that were happening to me.
I always wanted to be someplace else, someone else.
In being that I lost out on good moments and held on
to the bad ones.
Like I mentioned, I was in a different dimension.

Am I sober now?

too scared to be who I was
this is my new identity

I kind of miss that summer

I remember the sweltering summer,
the hope of something
yet to be realised.
The innocent dreams chased with enthusiasm,
of spending nights at your friend's house lying
around in her leather chair,
where tomorrow was not relevant,
it still hadn't hit us,

where everything was fine,
before we knew it wouldn't be.

COURAGE

i fought for you assuming you had a war to win

Still and rooted

Winter was hard,
cold and dry.
I stood there
still and rooted.
She thought I was dead
often looked at me with pity
but still thought I was beautiful.
She didn't know,
I was living, waiting,
for my time to bloom again;
and when I did,
she understood.

I saw her at the window
looking at me with admiration
as I stood still like I always did,
and she *whispered* "I am proud of you".

why can't I be happy

like a normal human being

Clarity

As you're moving forward
I'm going back.
You reach out to the future
as I turn away.
Slowly, I walk to a path different than yours
hoping I'd have the courage to meet you there someday.

I'm tired of running around,
I want to rest,
sit, write, dream again.
Do all the things that once made me complete.

even though i didn't know back then
i feel the emptiness today

A gentle flame of hope

Like a gentle flame of hope,
you come when I have no dream in my eyes.
Like a warm caress
you tell me i'll be fine.
I constantly get up and fall again,
yet your voice never change.
Like the light,
you find me at my darkest end.

i chase fireflies in the dark
trying to show you what i see

Solely me

Some things are just for me,
no one has to understand it.
Because if they did,
then my essence of being solely me
would get disrupted.

my walls have finally crumbled
so peacefully
i didn't feel a thing

Acceptance

A point where nothing flutters you,
a point where you barely manage a modest smile,
you take everything as is without an inch of you getting involved,
and yet, you have never been more content, more closer to
yourself.
Where you watched the sunset without admiration
but still felt pleasant,
unaware about the things that don't really matter,
you have never been truer.

don't think
just be

Norm

Nothing has to be the way it is supposed to be.
Feel what you feel.
If it moved you,
it will move someone too.

the tenderness of love that i'm discovering now
i should've known long ago

A word

Nature does not resist. It gracefully changes with the weather. It obeys the laws of time. Nothing goes against it.

Maybe we can learn from it too. Not resisting the inevitable but simply persisting until time comes our way again.

Knowing when to wait, knowing when its time.

i always wondered
how people could be
so close to each other

i never had that

Opinion

I don't have a lot to say.
I'm fine with people not knowing me.
No explanations, no points proven.
I don't have a lot to say.

my soul stopped speaking to me   now i have no one to turn to

Liberation

Letting go feels good.
You no longer feel the anxiety to be anything.
You are with yourself and you're okay with that.
Letting go feels like liberation,
liberating yourself.

licking my bruise like a cat
i healed myself with these words

Wholly

When will we live like ourselves
without anyone watching,
free from our own expectations
when will we lighten ourselves,
not being shy or fearful
when will we love ourselves,
so wholly, that we heal ourselves.

Just wait, and you will come to you.